BLUE WHALES

Julie Murray

Big Buddy Books

An Imprint of Abdo Publishing
abdobooks.com

abdobooks.com

Published by Abdo Publishing, a division of ABDO, PO Box 398166, Minneapolis, Minnesota 55439.
Copyright © 2020 by Abdo Consulting Group, Inc. International copyrights reserved in all countries.
No part of this book may be reproduced in any form without written permission from the publisher.
Big Buddy Books™ is a trademark and logo of Abdo Publishing.

Printed in the United States of America, North Mankato, Minnesota
052019
092019

THIS BOOK CONTAINS
RECYCLED MATERIALS

Design: Sarah DeYoung, Mighty Media, Inc.
Production: Mighty Media, Inc.
Editor: Liz Salzmann
Cover Photograph: iStockphoto
Interior Photographs: Craig Hayslip, Oregon State University Marine Mammal Institute/Flickr (p. 27);
        Francois Gohier/ardea.com (pp. 19, 24); iStockphoto (pp. 4–5, 9, 11, 12–13, 15, 17, 21, 28);
        Mark Carwardine/ardea.com (p. 23); Shutterstock (p. 7)

Library of Congress Control Number: 2018939652

Publisher's Cataloging-in-Publication Data
Names: Murray, Julie, author.
Title: Blue whales / by Julie Murray.
Description: Minneapolis, Minnesota : Abdo Publishing, 2020. I Series:
        Animal kingdom I Includes online resources and index.
Identifiers: ISBN 9781532116193 (lib.bdg.) I ISBN 9781532157684 (ebook)
Subjects: LCSH: Blue whale--Juvenile literature. I Whales--Juvenile literature. I
        Whales--Behavior--Juvenile literature. I Aquatic mammals--Juvenile
        literature. I Marine animals--Juvenile literature.
Classification: DDC 599.5248--dc23

Contents

LARGEST ANIMALS

Blue whales are the largest animals in the world. They are the biggest animals that ever lived.

Whales, dolphins, and porpoises are cetaceans. Cetaceans are **mammals** that live in the water. A cetacean has a tail, **flippers**, and one or two **blowholes**.

A blue whale is so big that its tongue alone weighs as much as an elephant!

Sea **mammals** are very different from fish. Fish have **gills** for breathing underwater. Instead of gills, mammals use **lungs** for breathing air. Whales and all other mammals cannot breathe underwater like fish.

What else do mammals have in common? Mammals are born alive instead of **hatching** from eggs. Mammals make milk for their babies to drink. **Apes**, horses, rabbits, and people are mammals too.

Cetaceans can be many sizes. Dolphins are much smaller than blue whales!

RORQUAL WHALES

>>>>>>>

There are many kinds of whales. There are sperm whales, beaked whales, white whales, and rorquals. Blue whales are rorquals.

Rorquals are whales with special folds, or **pleats**. These pleats are on the whale's underside. Whales **stretch** these pleats while feeding to make their mouths bigger.

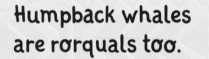

Humpback whales are rorquals too.

WHAT THEY LOOK LIKE

Blue whales are huge! A blue whale's heart is as large as a small car. These whales can be more than 90 feet (27 m) long. Adult blue whales may weigh more than 320,000 pounds (145,150 kg). Females grow larger than males.

Blue whales commonly swim about 12 miles an hour (19 kmh).

Sometimes barnacles grow on blue whales' flukes.

Blue whales are named after their blue-gray skin color. This smooth skin is spotted and white in places.

The blue whale has a large head and tail. Its tail has two fins, called flukes, that **jut** out sideways. The blue whale has a thin **flipper** on each side. It also has a small fin on its back.

The blue whale has two **blowholes** on top of its head. It takes in air and lets it out through its blowholes. Only a tiny bit of water **leaks** into the blowholes. The blue whale sprays out this water when it blows out air.

Blue whales can blow water 20 feet (6 m) into the air.

WHERE THEY LIVE

Blue whales swim in all the world's oceans. They commonly live in pairs or small groups.

Blue whales **migrate**. They travel thousands of miles in one year. Blue whales migrate to colder waters to eat.

They travel to warmer waters each year too. This is where blue whales are born. Many blue whales return to the same area year after year.

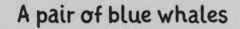

A pair of blue whales

Whale Songs

Blue whales make **moaning** sounds as they **migrate**. These sounds are the whales' "song." A blue whale's song can last as long as ten hours. Scientists believe male blue whales are calling out to females. A singing whale can be heard from 100 miles (161 km) away.

EATING

Blue whales can eat 5,000 pounds (2,268 kg) of food in one day. They eat a lot of krill. Krill are small sea animals.

Blue whales do not have teeth. These whales have **plates** of string-like **baleen** hanging inside their mouths. They use their baleen to catch food.

Whales, fish, birds, and other animals eat krill.

Baleen whales gulp a lot of food-filled water. The water escapes easily. But the food stays trapped among the baleen.

BLUE WHALE CALVES

>>>>>>

Baby whales are called calves. Female blue whales may have one calf every two or three years.

A newborn calf is between 20 and 25 feet (6 and 8 m) long. It weighs about 5,500 pounds (2,495 kg).

A blue whale calf stays close to its mother.

The oldest blue whale discovered by scientists lived to be around 110 years old!

Calves drink their mother's milk for seven or eight months. A blue whale calf can drink 100 gallons (379 l) each day. It also gains about 200 pounds (91 kg) each day.

Mother blue whales stay close and **protect** their calves. After a year or two, calves can live on their own. Blue whales may live as long as 70 years.

BLUE WHALES IN DANGER

At one time, hunting blue whales was common. People killed these sea **mammals** for their meat and **blubber**.

People have been hunting whales for centuries. Whales can also be hit and killed by ships.

Whale-watching is a popular activity in areas where blue whales are common.

Over the years, thousands of blue whales had been killed. They were in danger of dying out.

In 1966, special laws were passed to **protect** blue whales. Many countries agreed not to hunt them. This has helped. But blue whales are still **endangered**. There may be only 12,000 blue whales around today.

Glossary

ape—any of a group of tailless animals that are primates most closely related to humans. Gorillas and chimpanzees are apes.

baleen—a material hanging from the upper jaws of some kinds of whales. Whales use baleen to catch food.

blowhole—the opening on top of a whale's or dolphin's head used for taking in air.

blubber—fat underneath the skin of whales, dolphins, walruses, and other animals.

endangered—in danger of dying out.

flipper—a flat, paddle-shaped body part that whales, walruses, turtles, and dolphins use to swim.

gill—an organ that helps underwater animals breathe. It separates oxygen from water.

hatch—to be born from an egg.

jut—to stick out, up, or forward.

leak—to get into or out of something through a small crack or hole.

lungs—body parts that help the body breathe.

mammal—a member of a group of living beings. Mammals make milk to feed their babies and usually have hair or fur on their skin.

migrate—to move from one place to another to find food or have babies.

moaning—making a long, low sound.

plate—a thin, flat, stiff part or piece.

pleats—special folds that can open and close.

protect (pruh-TEHKT)—to guard against harm or danger.

stretch—to spread out to full size or greater.

Online Resources

Booklinks
NONFICTION NETWORK
FREE! ONLINE NONFICTION RESOURCES

To learn more about blue whales, please visit **abdobooklinks.com** or scan this QR code. These links are routinely monitored and updated to provide the most current information available.

Index